HOW? WHO? WHAT? WHEN? WHERE? WHY?

ABOUT
FISH AND SEA LIFE

CONTRIBUTORS

Alison Dickie
Bill Ivy
Jacqueline Kendel
Ann Langdon
Sheila Macdonald
Susan Marshall

Pamela Martin
Colin McCance
Nancy Prasad
Robin Rivers
Lois Rock

Jocelyn Smyth
Merebeth Switzer
Dave Taylor
Alison Tharen
Donna Thomson
Pam Young

INTERIOR ART AND DESIGN

Richard Comely
George Elliott

Greg Elliott
Ernie Homewood

Richard Migliore
Sue Wilkinson

First published in Canada
by Grolier Limited 1989
16 Overlea Blvd., Toronto, Ontario M5H 1A6
Telephone (416) 425-1924; Fax (416) 425-8858

Canadian Cataloguing in Publication Data

Questions kids ask about fish and sea life

(Questions kids ask ; 5)
ISBN 0-7172-2544-5 (bound) — ISBN 0-7172-2822-3 (pbk)

1. Fishes—Miscellanea—Juvenile literature.
2. Marine biology—Miscellanea—Juvenile literature.
3. Children's questions and answers. I. Smyth, Jocelyn.
II. Comely, Richard. III. Series.

QL617.2Q47   1988   j597   C89-093086-4

Paperback:
Cover design: Tania Craan
Cover art: Amanda Duffy

Casebound:
Cover design: Richard Comely
Cover art: Richard Comely

Questions Kids Ask . . . about FISH AND SEA LIFE

continued

What is the smallest fish?

The smallest fish in the world is the pygmy goby. A fully grown adult measures a mere 3 millimetres (1/8 of an inch)! This almost transparent fish makes its home in the freshwater streams and lakes of the Philippines. It also qualifies as the world's smallest vertebrate, or animal with a backbone.

What is a barracuda?

Barracuda are long, skinny, silver-gray fish that live in tropical waters. Most are about as long as you are tall but some grow to almost 2 metres (6 feet). They have very long, sharp teeth and they love bright, shiny things.

So if you ever go into waters where barracuda live, leave your jewelry behind. They might try to steal it—and take a bite out of you at the same time!

Do sharks attack people?

Sharks do attack people, but not nearly as often as books and movies would have you believe. While some sharks are powerful creatures with sharp teeth and strong jaws, others are shy and retiring and many are small.

If sharks do attack, they have reasons. A shark cannot swim backwards and is slow at turning, so it may attack a swimmer if it feels threatened. Or it may mistake a person for its fish dinner and take a bite, but it will usually swim away when it finds out the truth.

DID YOU KNOW . . . more people are killed by bee stings than by sharks!

How dangerous are piranhas?

Everyone has heard stories of people or animals being instantly devoured by piranhas. Just how vicious are these tiny terrors with the razor-sharp teeth?

In their natural environment in the Amazon River, piranhas rarely pay much attention to animals and people. They may take a little bite out of one that gets in their way, but as long as there are lots of small fish for them to eat they usually leave people and animals alone.

Piranhas tend to be vicious in captivity. In a fishtank, where space is limited, they will attack almost anything that is put in with them—including other piranhas.

How did the hammerhead shark get its name?

If you ever saw one, you wouldn't have to ask! The hammerhead shark's head is actually shaped like the head of a double-faced hammer, with an eye at either end.

This shark grows to over 5 metres (18 feet) long and lives in the warm waters of the Atlantic Ocean. It usually eats fish but will swallow anything it runs into—including tires and cans!

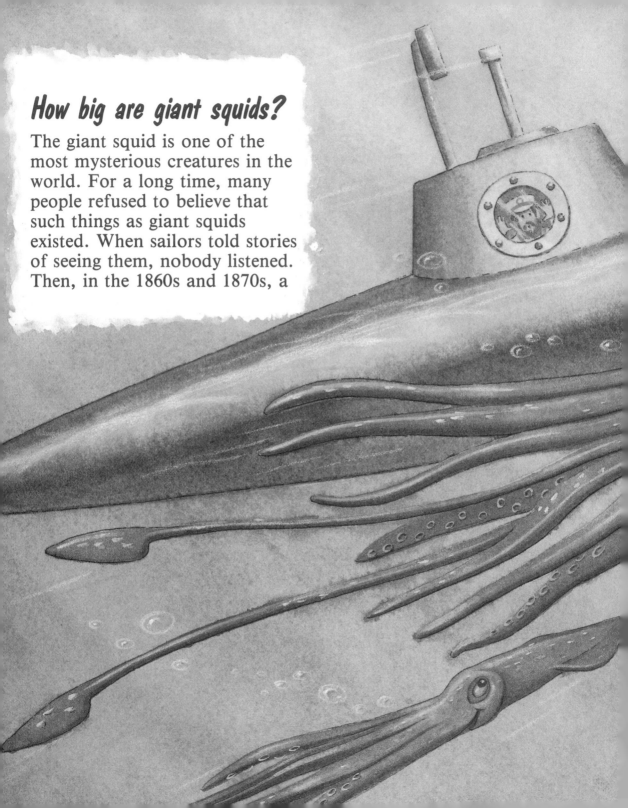

How big are giant squids?

The giant squid is one of the most mysterious creatures in the world. For a long time, many people refused to believe that such things as giant squids existed. When sailors told stories of seeing them, nobody listened. Then, in the 1860s and 1870s, a

series of dead giant squids washed up on beaches around the world. The biggest, found on a New Zealand beach, was almost 18 metres (60 feet) long from the end of its body to the tip of its long tentacles.

Nobody knows for sure how big a giant squid grows because they are rarely seen. Giant squids are eaten by sperm whales, which dive deep and may hunt the squids 3600 metres (12 000 feet) underwater. A squid's eight arms have suction cups, and these suckers leave scars on the heads of sperm whales. Some very big scars have been seen on whales, and because of this some people think that giant squids come much bigger than any yet found.

What is a crustacean?

Lobsters, shrimp, crabs and barnacles are crustaceans. They have a hard covering, or shell, segmented bodies, jointed legs and two pairs of antennae. Most live in water, but a few, such as wood lice, live on land.

There are about 30 000 species of shellfish ranging in size from 0.2 millimetres (8/1000 of an inch) to more than 3.6 metres (12 feet).

What is a hermit crab?

Normally, crabs are covered with a strong shell that protects their soft bodies. Hermit crabs aren't. Instead, they take over the empty shells of other creatures.

Hermit crabs can be found living in old snail, mussel or clam shells. They are called hermits because they live alone.

What is a sea horse?

Believe it or not, the sea horse is actually
a fish. It swims in an upright position,
propelling itself through the water with
a fin on its back. Sea horses live in
warm and temperate seas and vary
in size from 2 to 30 centimetres
(1 to 12 inches).

A sea horse's body is covered
with bony plates arranged in rings.
Its long tail is curved at the tip
and the sea horse uses it to attach
itself to seaweed or other
supports. But even more strange
than its appearance is the fact
that baby sea horses hatch in a
pouch in their father's belly.

Can starfish swim?

Despite its name the starfish is
not a fish, nor can it swim! It
can move though, thanks to
slender tubes called tube feet
under its arms. These feet are
tipped with suction cups which
grip hard surfaces and enable
the starfish to creep slowly
around.

DID YOU KNOW . . . if a
starfish loses an arm, it simply
grows a new one.

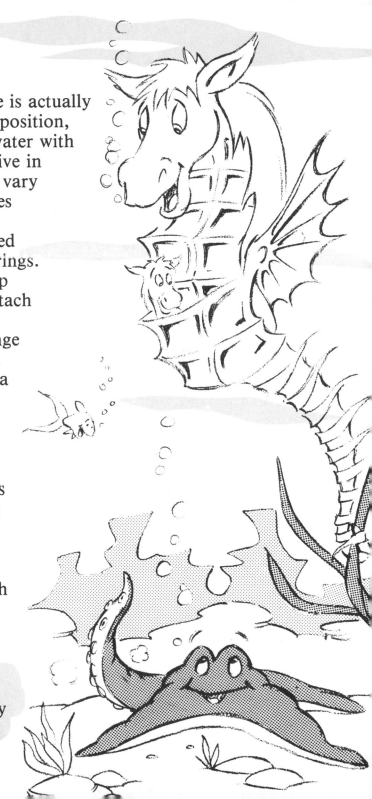

What is a pearl?

Pearls form when a piece of grit gets into an oyster's shell and irritates the oyster's insides. The oyster, which is all soft and slimy, starts to coat the scratchy piece of grit with clear, smooth material. This stuff hardens like glue. It is called nacre (which rhymes with acre or shaker).

Layer after layer of nacre is deposited around the grit, and a milky, hard, shiny ball is formed. This is a pearl. Pearls come in different shapes and colors. Most pearls are round and creamy white, but they can also have hints of yellow, green, pink, blue, brown or black. Black pearls are the rarest of all.

Most pearls are now cultivated. Bits of grit are put into oysters growing in nets that are hung under water until pearls have had time to form.

DID YOU KNOW . . . mussels and some types of clams also sometimes make pearls.

Can a clam eat a man?

On the coral reefs off the coasts of Indonesia live the biggest clams in the world. Called *Tridacna gigantea,* they may grow as long as 2 metres (6 feet) and weigh nearly 1000 kilograms (a ton).

They have been called "man-eating clams," but in truth they don't hunt people, and humans are not part of their diet.

However, like other clams, they have fleshy insides encased in hard shell jaws. If anything intrudes when these are open, they'll shut with a mighty snap, and people have been injured or even killed by accidentally stepping in one.

Can mussels move?

Mussels look rather like smooth, blue-black rocks, and they move around as much as a rock does —not at all!

Mussels are found in fresh and sea water. Some live partly buried in sand or mud. Others attach themselves to rock, docks or even each other by tough threads. The threads help keep them in place even when waves and currents are trying to move them around.

13

Are eels fish?

You might not think so to look at them, but eels are indeed fish.

The main difference between eels and other fish is that eels have long tube-like bodies and fewer fins. Most fish have two fins on their back and a tail fin to help them swim and to change direction. The two fins on the eel's back, however, have grown together, so it just has one big fin that runs all the way down its back to its tail.

What is an electric eel?

Electric eels are among the most feared fish in the world. They have long, tube-like bodies and can zap anything that gets in their way with an electrical shock strong enough to kill a horse!

Special organs inside the eel's body create the electrical charges. These organs make up almost half of the electric eel's body weight and can generate up to 550 volts. It isn't even necessary to touch an electric eel to get a shock from it. A fish that swims as far away as 60 centimetres (2 feet) may be stunned or killed by the electricity traveling in the water.

The electric eel uses its electricity for self-defense and to catch prey, such as frogs and small fish.

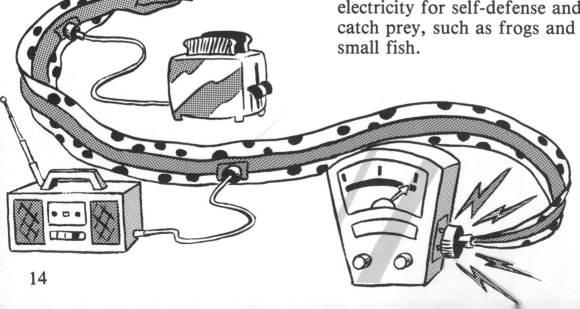

What is a jellyfish?

Despite its name the jellyfish is not a fish, nor would you want to eat it! This strange sea creature looks more like an umbrella made of jello than an animal. It has no skeleton at all, and looks flabby, but it is actually firm to the touch. Some types can propel themselves through the water by contracting their saucer-shaped form. Other types simply drift with the current.

There are over a thousand different kinds of jellyfish in the world. Some are no larger than a pea, while others are over 4 metres (13 feet) in diameter. They come in a variety of colors including white, pink, blue and brown. Many are completely transparent and a few are even phosphorescent, glowing mysteriously in the deep dark sea.

How do jellyfish sting?

Despite its harmless appearance the jellyfish is well armed. Its weapons are the numerous tentacles that hang from its body. Each is loaded with cells that produce a poison strong enough to paralyze small sea creatures. Once stung the helpless victims are held fast and later passed into the mouth of the jellyfish.

DID YOU KNOW . . . the sting of most jellyfish will not harm swimmers.

What is the fastest fish?

If you have ever tried to catch a pet goldfish or guppy with a net you know how fast a fish can swim. The champion speedster of them all is the sailfish. This living torpedo can travel at speeds of up to 95 kilometres (60 miles) per hour. That's as fast as a car speeds down a highway.

What is the world's largest fish?

When it comes to size no other fish can match the whale shark. Although this gentle giant feeds only on plankton and small fish, it can weigh more than two elephants! The largest specimen ever captured measured a whopping 18.5 metres (61 feet).

Now that is one whale of a fish!

Why do fish swim in schools?

Not because they want to learn. Not because they are lonely. And not because they enjoy playing follow the leader.

Various types of fish swim in groups known as schools with fish of the same size and species. Fish that travel in schools do so mainly as a defense against predators. It may also help them find food. The number of fish in a school varies from 25 for large fish to several thousand for small fish.

Why do squids squirt ink?

Squids have a very unusual way of defending themselves. When under attack they blow ink into the water through a tunnel behind their head. This blue-black fluid forms a "smoke screen" which is impossible to see through and may also interfere with a predator's sense of smell.

Some species use their ink in a different way. They squirt out a much thicker substance which forms into a blob about the same size as the squid itself. If all goes well the enemy attacks the blob instead of the squid and swims away with nothing more than a mouthful of ink!

What is a sea cucumber?

Did you think all cucumbers grew in gardens? Not a sea cucumber!

The sea cucumber is an animal that lives at the bottom of the sea. It gets its name from its long, cucumber-shaped body. The sea cucumber catches food with tentacles around its mouth. Some have tube feet and can crawl around; others simply bury themselves in the sand.

DID YOU KNOW . . . sea cucumbers are related to starfish and are found in oceans throughout the world.

Which fish carry their own lights?

Lanternfish, as the name suggests, give off their own pale blue or green light from spots on the surface of their body.

Lanternfish live in deep ocean waters but often come to the surface at night to eat. Insects are attracted to the light and fly close enough to the fish to be gobbled up. When underwater, the light can also attract small, tasty fish.

Some types of lanternfish use their light for self-defense. When a predator approaches, the light fades and then suddenly flashes. The attacking fish is blinded long enough for the lanternfish to make a quick getaway.

What sea creature looks like a flower?

What *is* that flower in the water? It looks like a cross between a sunflower and a big summer squash. Yipes—it just ate a small fish!

That "flower" is really an animal called a sea anemone.

Sea anemones may be green, purple, blue or red. They have feet like suction cups and they like to stand on rocks. They don't move much, yet they can still catch small fish thanks to their string-like tentacles. These are covered with poison that can paralyze a fish. The anemone then uses its tentacles to pull fish into its mouth in the center.

Can any fish live out of water?

Although all fish are water creatures, some can actually live out of water for a long time.

The lungfish normally lives in shallow waters in Australia and South America. But during the summertime, most of the water dries up, leaving a few small puddles and big patches of mud.

In order to survive, lungfish dig holes in the mud and bury themselves. They then make a moist, mucousy sack that they live in at the bottom of the hole until the rains come in the fall.

If the rains don't come, a lungfish can stay in its hole for up to four years!

Can a perch go for a walk?

On a rainy day in some parts of the world, you might see a fish out walking. You would be looking at a climbing perch.

Climbing perch have much stronger fins than other perch and use them to crawl over land. The fins also have strong spines on them that help them move.

The reason these fish go onto land is to get to a new waterhole. If they can't find one, they bury themselves in the mud and wait for rain.

How many fish are there in the sea?

Scientists estimate that there are more than 22 000 different *kinds* of fish in the world—more than all of the varieties of mammals, birds and reptiles put together. With so many kinds of fish living in so many different places, it is impossible to count exactly how many fish there are in the sea.

How can you tell the age of a fish?

What do fish and trees have in common? Both have growth rings that tell us their age.

In summer, food is plentiful and a fish's scales grow quickly, forming rings similar to those in a tree trunk. In winter, the fish aren't as active and eat less. The scales do not grow as quickly, and the rings form dark bands. Counting these bands tells how many winters the fish has lived.

How do fish breathe?

Like all animals fish need oxygen to live. However, they take it out of the water, rather than the air.

Fish take in water by mouth. The water then passes through their gills, where the oxygen is absorbed into the bloodstream. The water then leaves through a slit on each side of the head.

Are sponges plants or animals?

Sponges look like plants. Some look like branching trees, others are thin and flat like moss and some are round masses like shrubs. But sponges are actually animals even though they have no eyes, ears, mouth, heart, stomach or nervous system.

The main reason that sponges are classified as animals is because of the way they feed. They don't make their own food, like green plants do. Sponges capture their food. The body of a sponge is covered with tiny pores. Little plants and animals flow into the pores and then enter a system of water canals in the sponge's body. Once inside, the food is digested and the same canal system carries away the waste. You can say sponges are like living sieves.

DID YOU KNOW . . . most of the so-called sponges sold in stores today aren't true sponges. They're synthetic materials made to look like animal sponges.

Does a parrotfish really look like a parrot?

It can't fly and it can't "talk" like a parrot, yet a parrot is the first thing that comes to mind when you see this fish.

Like their namesake, parrotfish tend to be brightly colored and their scales appear to overlap in the same way as a bird's feathers.

Moreover, as a parrotfish ages, its head changes. The forehead and front of the face above the mouth bulge out until they look like the top of a parrot's beak.

Parrotfish eat the creatures that live inside coral reefs.

How long do goldfish live?

The modest goldfish has sure come a long way. Originally from southern China it is now a favorite pet all around the world. Initially the goldfish was not gold—wild specimens still living today are brownish green. Through special breeding their color and shape have been changed dramatically.

If you are the proud owner of a goldfish, your pet could live up to 17 years.

DID YOU KNOW . . . there are even goldfish shows, where prizes are awarded for new varieties. Not bad for a fish which is little more than a glorified carp.

What is an octopus?

Despite its frightening appearance, the octopus is a timid creature with a highly developed brain. It has a soft bag-shaped body and eight arms, or tentacles. Each one is lined with a row of suckers that give the octopus a very tight grip. It has two large, shiny eyes and a beak-like mouth. It ranges in size from 30 centimetres (1 foot) to almost 9 metres (30 feet).

The octopus can swim but usually moves by crawling along the ocean floor. When chased by an enemy it squirts a black ink into the water, forming a dense cloud that hides it from view.

DID YOU KNOW . . . the octopus has another means of self defense: it can change color to blend in with its surroundings. Now you see it— now you don't.

Can two fish have one body?

Certain little fish of the *Ceratidae* family have a unique arrangement: the female carries her mate attached to her head! The fish are called black seadevils, and they live in the darkest depths of the ocean.

At first glance the male looks like an appendage to the head of the female, but it's really a fish breathing through its own gills. Shortly after hatching, the male seeks out a female and clamps onto her with his teeth. He stays there for the rest of his life. Their outer skin connects and their blood systems become one.

The wife is the sole supporter of this family. She not only supplies the transportation, but all the food as well. Digested food passes through their singular blood system. The male is fed without ever having to open his mouth!

What is the biggest fish in the Great Lakes?

Some very big fish live in the Great Lakes and their connecting waterways. The muskellunge and the northern pike can grow to 2 metres (6 feet) long and weigh up to 32 kilograms (70 pounds). A record lake trout was caught that weighed over 45 kilograms (100 pounds), but it was a freak. Large lake trout usually weigh 18 kilograms (40 pounds) or so. Channel catfish can reach that weight, and so can carp.

What is a sardine?

Most of us know sardines only as small, oily fish that come in tightly packed cans from the store. Sardines are popular as a snack food and many fisherman use them as bait when they are trying to catch tuna or cod.

The fish in sardine cans are not always the same kind of fish. They may be young herring or almost any other gray- or silver-colored fish that are 10 to 20 centimetres (4 to 8 inches) long.

But is there a true sardine?

Yes. A true sardine is a young pilchard—another small, gray fish popular among fish lovers.

But the biggest of the lake fish by far is the lake sturgeon. Sturgeon are long, torpedo-shaped fish covered in bony plates. They feed on the bottom of lakes and commonly grow to be 2.5 metres (8 feet) long, weighing in excess of 45 kilograms (100 pounds).

What sort of creatures live in the deep sea?

Most of the sea animals we know live in the upper layer of the oceans, in the top 180 metres (600 feet). Below that, extending to the bottom that lies 3600 metres (12 000 feet) deep or more, is the region of deep sea life.

Not much light penetrates below the upper layer and so no plankton can live there because it needs sunlight to grow. Life is not abundant in the deep sea, but there is some, and it includes many bizarre forms that are uniquely adapted to the world they live in. There are fish with huge eyes and others with great

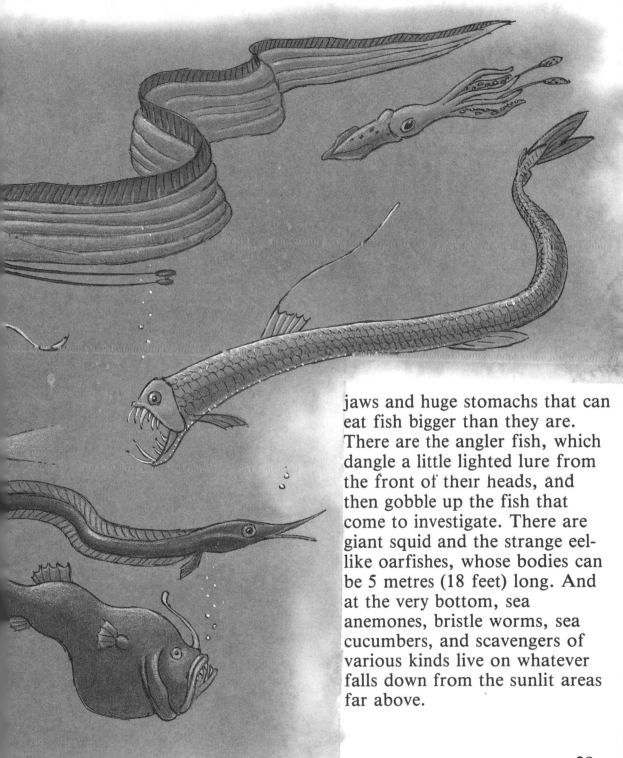

jaws and huge stomachs that can eat fish bigger than they are. There are the angler fish, which dangle a little lighted lure from the front of their heads, and then gobble up the fish that come to investigate. There are giant squid and the strange eel-like oarfishes, whose bodies can be 5 metres (18 feet) long. And at the very bottom, sea anemones, bristle worms, sea cucumbers, and scavengers of various kinds live on whatever falls down from the sunlit areas far above.

29

How does a salmon return to the same river to spawn?

Salmon are born in the upper areas of large rivers. When they are two to four years old, they swim down the river to live in the ocean. They stay there for one to three years, then go back to the river they came from to lay their eggs.

Salmon may have to travel almost 5000 kilometres (3000 miles) to the river they came from. Many scientists think the fish first find their way to the coast by sensing the earth's magnetic field. Then their sense of smell guides them. Each river has its own special smell and the salmon recognizes the one that smells like home!

Can you smell *your* way home?

DID YOU KNOW . . . most salmon die after spawning only once, but some Atlantic salmon live to return to the sea and come home again to spawn a second time.

Index _____